When the Winter Whispers
Tales of Agony

Navyansh Sharma

About the Poet

Navyansh Sharma is a writer of silence, and an advocate of finding meaning in terror. With a pen dipped in darkness, he crafts narratives which blur the line between myth and madness. His writings explore themes of emotional dread, existential terror, and the quiet nature of life's journey. When not wandering the icy wastelands, you might find him sitting in a dark locus, where silence is all you hear.

'When the Winter Whispers Tales of Agony' is his debut anthology. It is a chilling tribute to the beauty of ruin, the ache of memory, and the whispers that echo long after hope has faded.

About the Tale

In a world where ice has desolated all that exists, a nameless wanderer embarks on a journey. His journey, prompted by his lust for knowledge, took him across kingdoms, haunting ruins, and sacred treasures. In his search for meaning, he uncovers a fragment of a lost reality; where gods have fallen, time has broken, and where whispers carry frozen damnation.

Guided by ancient relics, the Runestone of the Lost Continuum, The Blade of Winter's Curse, the Cloak of frozen shade, and more, he finds his reality to be a shattered mirror, one which reflects a demented truth. The ones who are the creators of those relics are far older than the Gods we are familiar with. He meets a mysterious gladiator, one who bears the Blade of Winter's Curse, and uncovers the sigil which seals his fate. The protagonist spirals into a terrifying truth, one where hope is a betrayal, purpose is an illusion, and where salvation exacts a cost too great to bear.

A tale woven by myth, horror and sorrow, and philosophical despair, When the Winter Whispers Tales of Agony is a haunting journey through cosmic dread and inner ruin. It is not a story of triumph, but of a soul consumed by frost, left to whisper his pain for eternity.

Whispers of Gratitude

Every winter has witnesses. This book is mine.

To the cold dark nights, and to the hazy zephyrs; Thank You.

This book was born in the cold: of winter, of longing, and of the quiet corners of the heart, where agony brews.

I thank winter, not just as a season, but as a presence. It whispered these verses into being, wrapped in frost and shadow. I thank the emotions that spilled: grief, wonder, yearning, and love, for they bled into every stanza.

And to the one who unknowingly lit the first spark, like a light in the night, you were the hush that steadied my chaos. You know who you are. This book would not have been written without your silence, and your magic. To all those who wander through their own winters: may these whispers keep you company.

To Winter,
Who wrapped me in silence,
Whose cold gave me comfort,
And the one who watched me bleed
Poetry into the snow.
Only in your still I heard
What the world tried to drown.

To Darkness,
Who saw my sorrow and suffering,
Who is the alibi to my change,
And the one who inspired me to be soft.
Only through your love,
Could my soul ever be as of depth,
As it is now.

To the Warmth of My Cold Days,
Who sounded as a gentle whisper,
You were not my muse,
But you became the pulse behind my words.
You are the reason this book exists.
You are the reason I listened
When the winter whispered.

The Winter Whispers Curses of the Heat

I often converse in solitude,
A solitude where I'm not so alone.
My dear winter lingers to listen.
She hears everything I say.

Rarely does she talk back to me,
And when she does,
She whispers with a ghoul's haunting.
She whispers curses;
Curses of a darkened sword.

She talks of heat's indifference.
She says that he burns;
Burns the flames of
Hope and despair alike.
She leaves me to wonder,
'How can her contrary be
So malevolent at heart?'

I ask her why heat is as so,
But she never answers.
I then tell her to let go of the hate,
She has let exist for so long.
She listens, but again doesn't respond.
I ask why she is so, and once again,
The winter whispers curses of the heat.

The Night Yearns for my Presence

Every night,
As I sit on the old chair,
Left to rot on the rooftop,
The night sings to me.
With her cool winds whistling past,
And the leaves of trees rustling,
She sings songs of sorrow.

The winds speak of a kingdom,
The stars speak of frozen souls.
The night speaks of a winter cursed,
The constellations of a frostfallen.

The night, she often calls out to me.
She beckons with the light
From the Moon and Constellations.
Cassiopeia tells me about love, and
Gemini speaks of her woe.
They are like my sisters,
Forever following me,
All through the night

I talk to my only brother,
The Moon, often.
He goes to his love every month,
But never tells me about her.
I think he loves darkness as I do,
For in his absence,
I am left alone with her.

When the Darkness was Lit

I lived in the comforting darkness,
Until light invaded my home.
I lived in a place of cradle and caress,
When the blinding light stole it away.

May the light be dark,
And not invade other homes.
I faced torment, as the light shone
With the beams of
Growth and knowledge.

My emotions then betrayed me,
And imprisoned my soul within my mind.
Allow me freedom from agony.
Allow me freedom.
Then was the change brought.
The light is tormenting.
It is uncomfortable.
I need my darkness back.
Call the winds which carry
The ash of my forlorn self.
Take me back to before
The Darkness was lit.

Whispers of an Enchantress

You give life meaning.
You make existence worth something.
You make living beautiful,
And give time its power.

Don't be afraid
of the power you possess,
Or rather; the beauty.
For you are gorgeous
from head to toe;
To luminesce with the shine
Of the souls you have reaped.

Your face
Glitters more than
The sky at night.
Are you what souls look like:
An everlasting collection
Of darkness and stardust.

You bear the lustre
From the echoing screams,
Which linger
With anger and apathy alike.
Your voice resonates
Like a nightingale's song,
Echoing the gifts of life;
Which have allowed you
This sound of an enchantress.

And when death,
You'll knock on my door;
I'll embrace you, with open arms.
Like a man does,
With his wife,
On a cold winter night,
Where even snow
Feels cold, and when
Even ice shivers.

Betrayed by Belief

A man stands lost on a foggy road,
Neither the end, nor the beginning in sight.
He still treads, with all he has.
Who gave him this strength?
It wasn't anger, neither was sorrow.
Love told me that
She hadn't brought strength to him.
Who was it, then?
Maybe it was just you all along;
Giving way to the lost.

My friend, you lie.
You help the helpless;
You allow them life again.

Your deception is cruel,
Nay, it is divisive.
Why do you add chapters to stories?
Why, with such passion, do you deny denouement?

My dear friend, you are malevolent.
You are the greatest of all liars,
And the worst of all betrayers.
Withdraw yourself from others,
Allow only the strong to exist.

You are demented, my friend Hope.
You are cruel, my friend Hope.
Your wailing whispers,
And your caring caress,
Both are unfeeling by themselves.
Be exiled to that locus,
Where the cries of the unheard overheard,
And the cries of the sorrowed happy,
All echo, in the indifferent halls.

No one ever told me that
Hope was supposed to be
the truth.

I Hope to See You Again

When I'm sitting in my veranda,
A slight tear falls from my eye.
I read the letters I wrote for you,
And on that dark snowy night,
I hope to see you again.

When I'm lying on my bed,
A lingering thought comes to my mind.
I look at the gifts I had bought for you,
And at that cold winter midnight,
I hope to see you again.

When I'm lying on my roof,
A tremor starts in my hands.
I think about the life I wanted for you,
And at that cold snowy dead of night,
I hope to see you again.

I really do, my love.
I hope to see you again.
For one last time,
I hope to see you again.
For another chance at love,
I hope to see you again.
For a longing that was never fulfilled,
I hope to see you again.

The Frost has Frozen the Holy Land

I walked the lands to the north,
And I came across a kingdom;
One forgotten by maps
And by cartographers of the present.
The castle was made of ice,
And the walls of frost.
The daylight shone haze,
As the sky lit the land in snow.

"Greetings, lost traveller.
Welcome to this dead instance.
Leave at this moment,
Or indifference will freeze
Reality as you know it."

I then heard a spectral call,
As I stared at the frozen hall.
I was directed towards a locus,
When time's end meets
Reality's desolation.
All while the living dead are
Greeted by the dead living.

The Runestone of the Lost Continuum

I talked to the stars,
They flickered with the weight of regret.
I asked them about their powers;
And they showed me an obsolete object.
I looked at the metallic body,
Which resembled those ailing stars.
I heard a strange whisper from the artifact,
As the winds carried the weight of the Universe.
That rune I received was ravaged.
I held in my hands a strange object,
And as I stood in that foreign field
I was holding a fragment of the Universe.
I didn't know yet, but I was holding
The Runestone of the Lost Continuum.

Monolith of the Eternal Winter

The stone I held emitted a silent whisper.
Was it trying to show me the way to something?
Or was the rune reminiscing secrets of winter?
I heard its call.
The frozen water will have a longing left. Perhaps
The frozen rain carries an ache.
I woke them up.
Greet the lost souls here. They too froze.
And as I walked following the path destined,
I saw a shadow stalking my steps.
As I looked, my tears froze.
I was at the locus, where frost meets ice,
And where even vapour freezes.
My eyes cast light upon the stone,
And my bones froze in place.
The rune said that it was
The Monolith of the Eternal Winter.

Cloak of the Frozen Shade

I continued away from the titanstone,
With a shattering will,
And crumbling bones and heart.
He is watching. He is feeling.
"The frozen kingdom had a conqueror.
His kingdom was invaded by a grim gladiator.
He is beyond this world,
Beyond realities, and beyond time.
Ice was his demise."
The runestone keeps secrets.
Who is he?
I came to the monolith.
'There's nothing here.
"The ghoul will etch haunting,
Let him."
He has a hand of frozen fire.
He gave me his cloak.
It was the cool shade from the ice,
But the darkness is dead.
When the ghoul sounded, he left
The Cloak of the Frozen Shade.
He is watching. He is feeling.

The Blade of Winter's Curse

Horror may tread this path.
The ghoul was haunting.
His shadows bring terror,
And his voice, fright.
The undead are here,
With shrieking voices and
Haunting howls,
They follow me.
"Stop. You'll drown in ice."
The frozen haze hides me,
The tides are low.
The snow is torment.
The cloak radiates frozen heat,
As the towering stone casts its shadow on me.
The frozen haze hides me.
'Is that a weapon of the gods?'
"Don't go near. He is fear.
He'll destroy everything,
If you dare touch it."
I held the sword,
The Blade of the Winter's Curse.
The undead are here,
With shrieking voices and
Haunting howls,
They follow me.
"Stop. You'll drown in ice."

Scroll of the Great Temptation

It's getting harder to walk.
The frozen water is getting deeper.
They are still here and so is he.
Still watching, and still feeling.
The undead caged me. He is here.
Locked behind bars I stand,
My horror spills out as fading screams.
"Cease your walk, or
Face the eternal consequence."
The blade tore through the ice,
Ice is roaring in the sky.
When the haze settled, I saw.
I'm in a chamber of torment,
But why are there inhuman bones here?
They are still here and so is he.
Still watching, and still feeling.
I hear screams and moans,
The runestone is now shining bright.
I had a vision.
"Stop."
The runestone keeps secrets.
I see a scroll on that rock.
"Cease your walk, or
Face the eternal consequence.
That's the Scroll of the Great Temptation."
'Why are these bones moving?'

The Wand Which Whispers Winter

The body with no nose breathes,
And with no flesh lives.
He opens his gaping maw to speak.
"Greetings, lost traveller.
Welcome to this dead instance.
Leave at this moment,
Or indifference will freeze
Reality as you know it."
The runestone flies to his grasp.
Where is the sword,
If not pierced into my heart?
The cloak's warmth is foreign.
"I am the Gladiator,
Whose death was called
Impossible by the books and scrolls.
When frost invaded my conquest,
I was defeated and cast out here.
I am the keeper of this lost scroll."
I had a vision.
"Only a being of flesh
Can give my dreams reality.
Take the scroll, and
Freeze the ice,
Melt the fire that no longer rains on this world.
The Wand Which Whispers Winter,
Waits for the hand that dares
To change what cannot be changed."

Sigil of the Frostfallen

My eyes are burning.
"The ritual needs a sigil.
As long as ice exists in this world,
I cannot fulfill my destiny.
Take my sword,
And the fire within my frozen heart,
Shatter the ice which reigns on this world.
My heart has a cursed spell,
It's the sigil of my existence;
Sigil of the Frostfallen."
I wield the wand and read the scroll,
I chant the spell and pray.
I take the blade in my hands,
The ice trembles as water.
I pierce the Earth's skin deep.
The world trembled in agony.
And then it started to snow,
The land froze again.
Reality froze, time froze, and so did darkness.
The runestone stopped glowing, and
The cloak burned into ice.
The wand shatters into snowflakes and
The scroll tears with torment.
The blade then shatters.
Why did the rune turn to dust?
This is the lost continuum,
And I am caged: Beyond this world,
And beyond time.
Thus is my fate sealed.

God is worse than man. Atleast man listens. Atleast man responds. God doesn't respond. He stops listening in the midst of adversity. "God is omnipotent", that is what we have been told. How is God omnipotent if justice begs for hearing, and victims plead for mercy.

Maybe we have been answered, within the insignificance of our momentary lives. Are human lives worth God's saving? We live so we can die. Our life is not a journey, it is a gravestone being dug. Maybe humans should accept indifference. Maybe, just maybe, God really has left us to end.

The Gods are Gone, the Old Ones Remain

The Gods,
Where are they?
Why is ice overpowering?
Are gods nonexistent to protect,
What they so proudly call theirs?

"Once temples stood like the monolith,
But the winds have torn them apart.
A hollow throne somewhere
Stands in ruin,
Longing for its destined heart.
The Gods have been silenced
But the old ones whisper still.
They are left to live and linger,
They are the forces we bow to."

Gods are immortal,
How can they see defeat?
Are no mortals ringing the church bells?
The sirens are sounding,
Why are they asleep?
'Are Gods dead?'

"Once temples stood like the monolith,
But the winds tore them apart.
The throne still stands in ruin.
The gods have been frozen,
But the old ones linger still.
They are left to live and linger,
They are the forces we become."

The Great Ancient One

The runestone was ancient,
And the first lead to my doom.
Who made it whisper?
Who filled its veins?
I held the lost continuum.
Its light was no light at all.

"He was watching, he was feeling."

And then I heard a spectral rustle,
As if the void felt my ribs.
My bones started to quake,
And my skull began to break.

"He was watching, he was feeling.
I was the ghoul there.
The ruler of the kingdom is ancient.
He is beyond strength. Ice is his power.
He watches, but he does not blink."

I was a mere wanderer,
What had I to give?
He is beyond reality,
Why did he wail?

"He is everywhere,
He is still watching.
His ice spreads like fire.
I was the first fallen, and
You walked my path.
The hunt for forbidden knowledge,
That's what wrote our doom.
He is the great ancient one.
I may be beyond realities,
Yet his strength is beyond compare.
His power is not force but silence.
Not a fire burning, but the frost seeping.
He does not strike. He waits.
And waiting is worse."

Cathedral of the Frozen

A vision stalking these lands
Crept up in my head.
It was haunting and torment;
A place of surrender and slumber.
Power was not foreign there,
It was divine.
The winds were frozen gold,
And the statues, frozen gems.

Some statues were howling,
In a great silent agony.
Others were weeping,
From their withering eyes,
Tears which never fell.
Why were there frozen statues?
I had a shiver from the frost,
Or as the silent screams deafened me,
I looked at the halls.
They were not mere statues,
They were our prayers turned into ice.
They were the gods we begged for mercy,
But even they fell to ice.

The Winter Void

I have reached the heart of these lands,
Where the ice is the deepest,
And the winds are the coldest.
The haze blurs my vision,
Like a bright white veil to the sky.
Why can I hear voices?
And as I walk farther,
These voices are getting louder.
I hear dead souls begging, pleading.
The frozen souls sing curses of heat.
I can hear silent sounds of whispers,
What are they whispering of?

I heard a man a long while ago warn;
"In the land of doom,
Do not try to linger.
The doomsday is near. Fear.
Fear the unknown,
It'll write your demise.
Bathe in curiosity, and you'll roll the world,
Blinding all that exists.
Halt life. Accept. Embrace."

The ice has forgotten,
Me ever being separate from it.
My name is fading,
My vision is fading,
And so is my memory.
My past is long gone.
Only the ice remains.
The frost whispers something.

Tale of the First Frost

I listen with curious ears,
What the ice has to say:
"The world was tender,
Trees lush and lands green.
Silence however, was hungry.
It slowly crept into the dark nights,
Until the daytime too,
Flourished with my torment.
The wind does not howl; It grieves.
I am power.
The old gods joined powers,
But the ritual seemed to fail.
The Gods used my strength.
What they did not realise
Was the cost of existence itself.
They froze the world,
Looped time for eternity.
A throne in the far North
Whispers for a ruler;
A man of great wisdom.
Your salvation is at hand,
But it exacts a heavy toll."

Hollow Kings

The ice told me a grave secret.
With my shaking bones,
I made the journey to that locus,
Where the throne of the wise longs.
I looked at the golden-blue metal,
With frozen gems shining like stars.
And as my jaw trembled
With the haunting cold,
I found it harder to take a step,
As I moved forward.
I felt a pull away from salvation.
I reached the throne,
My remaining mortal drained.
The crow's call gave me shivers.
As I got closer and closer,
The pull away instead became
A pull inwards.
My will didn't play a role.
I sat on the throne then.
And when I did, it wasn't me anymore.
I felt a strange pull on my ribs,
The world blurred into silence.
And then nothing else
Seemed so significant.
As i stepped out from my damnation,

The ice called out to me.
"Fool. You are no wise man, but
A weak man in search
Of a long lied truth.
Your soul has thus been stripped
Of whatever remains of that body.
Your wailing whispers shall be heard,
By the ones who precede you.
And together with your past,
Rule over all that has been damned."

The Damned Melodies

I walked through the silent path,
And then I saw myself in a reflection.
The traitor who betrayed me,
Looked back at me with agony.
I then heard a sound that alarmed me.
A sound like a village chant,
Though the sound carried no warmth.
My mind is fading. They are spirits.
I hear the abyss calling out to me,
Like the night once did, all that time ago.
A place of eternity but torment,
A hymn of peace but agony.
The undead dead are here,
With their shrieking voices and
Haunting howls,
They are frozen in my anguish.
I feel a pull towards their hymn,
A will to sing for eternity.
Hollowed existence is rare;
It is a gift.
I will not stop to sing
The damned melodies.

A Purpose Without Hope

In this world where silent whispers
Linger like twinkling stars in the night,
The journey to find a purpose
Becomes quite insignificant.

Life exists as mere energy,
While the physical ones are frozen.
The old ones dream and judge.
They exist to control,
And nothing beyond.

The gladiator serves the old ones,
Every bone in his being
Is under control of those old ones.
Bridging the great gap
Between our physical and
Their ethereal existence.

The Gods are left to weep.
Wail and whisper for eternity.
Their defeat to ice tormented them.
And now,
The Gods wait for their savior,
One who will free them from
The bondage of ice.

Some exist as the undead,
Who have now been caged by ice.
They are doomed to sing,
And to accept their fate.
Only then can they be at peace.

In this brokenness,
I, much like in my human life,
Struggle to find a purpose.
I am a being wandering,
And nothing beyond.
I however, pity those
Who sought a meaning,
And found only frost.
How great it is, not to seek
A purpose without hope.

My Fear Endured Another Winter

Knowledge is a weapon,
But a weapon too strong
Often leads to desolation.
The abyss called out to me,
My answer soon became
The handle of the sword
With which I stabbed myself.

I sought answers to forbidden questions,
And the universe answered with ruin.
I have wandered these snowy lands,
For months or years.
My winter is almost over.
I look at the ice,
Which looks back to me,
And I feel pity at the being staring back.
Human life is beautiful,
It does not need a great purpose.
Happiness lies in what is, and
The 'could be' will be the ink of despair.

I am beyond salvation now,
Without a power guiding me,
And without hope,
Through this apocalypse. I am lost.
I am now living in the story I wrote.
The frost is slowly consuming me.
My fears stand greater than ever.
I came seeking solace,
But I found ruin.
Soon I will fall, losing my being.
However, in my final breath, I will know;
My fear endured another winter.

The Winter Whispers Tales of Agony

I stand in a foreign land,
It is still a bit cold here.
The blinding haze lingers,
Stalking like a shadow.
I heard the lingering whisper, as
The winter whispers tales of agony.

I feel a great power here,
A weight like the one
Near those archaic relics.
I see those old judges,
In slumber, and dreaming.

I see him,
He is still watching,
And is still feeling.
As he opens his maw to speak,
My mind crumbles into madness.
The winter whispers tales of agony.

The words he left broke me;
Left me in tormenting agony.
The salvation really is at hand,
It demands comfort for existence.
Souls shall be free; gods shall rule.
However, the torment of these souls;
It shall take the form of ghosts,
And will haunt the tormented.

The choice was mine.
To torment beings with ice, or
To torment beings with fear.
Was comfort worth existence,
Or would existence be incomplete?
The whispers grow louder now,
I hear the cold breath.
It calls my name, as promises release.
The price is a thousand lifetimes,
Of haunting this broken world.
To leave, to let go, and to walk away;
Would I escape, or simply add
Another layer to the torment?
To bear the frost, or to bear the fear,
What am I to do when salvation itself
Is a double-edged sword in hand?

Therefore, I stand defeated.
Not a man, but a memory,
Reminiscing my forlorn self.
Whispering the tales of agony,
For the winter will not let go.
It never does. Again and again,
The winter whispers tales of agony.

Now, I realise.
The winter is an ache.
The winter endures for eternity.
Its whispers stalk the ears
Of those who dare to listen.
Remember:
If the winter calls out to you,
Turn away.
Do not hear the voice.
Let silence remain.
For to listen is to lose
What never truly was yours.